Foods of Spain

Barbara Sheen

KIDHAVEN PRESS

An imprint of Thomson Gale, a part of The Thomson Corporation

THOMSON
————————
GALE

Detroit • New York • San Francisco • New Haven, Conn. • Waterville, Maine • London

For more information, contact
KidHaven Press
27500 Drake Rd.
Farmington Hills, MI 48331-3535
Or you can visit our Internet site at http://www.gale.com

LIBRARY OF CONGRESS CATALOGING-IN-PUBLICATION DATA

Sheen, Barbara.
 Foods of Spain / by Barbara Sheen.
  p. cm. — (A taste of culture)
 Includes bibliographical references and index.
 ISBN: 978-0-7377-3539-0 (hardcover)
 1. Cookery, Spanish—Juvenile literature. I. Title.
 TX723.5.S7S52 2007
 641.5946—dc22
 	
                                                                      2007021907

ISBN-10: 0-7377-3539-2

Printed in the United States of America

Contents

Fresh Healthy Ingredients

Spanish cooking is simple and delicious. It relies on fresh local ingredients for its clean natural flavor. Since Spain is blessed with a temperate climate, rich soil, and a long coastline, Spaniards have an abundance of fine ingredients to choose from. Tomatoes, potatoes, eggs, rice, wheat, chicken, pork, game, and cheese all find their way into Spanish dishes. But it is olive oil, garlic, and seafood and fish that give Spanish cooking its distinct flavor and make it one of the healthiest **cuisines** in the world.

Ancient Oil

Olive oil has been an essential part of the Spanish diet for centuries. The ancient Phoenicians planted the first

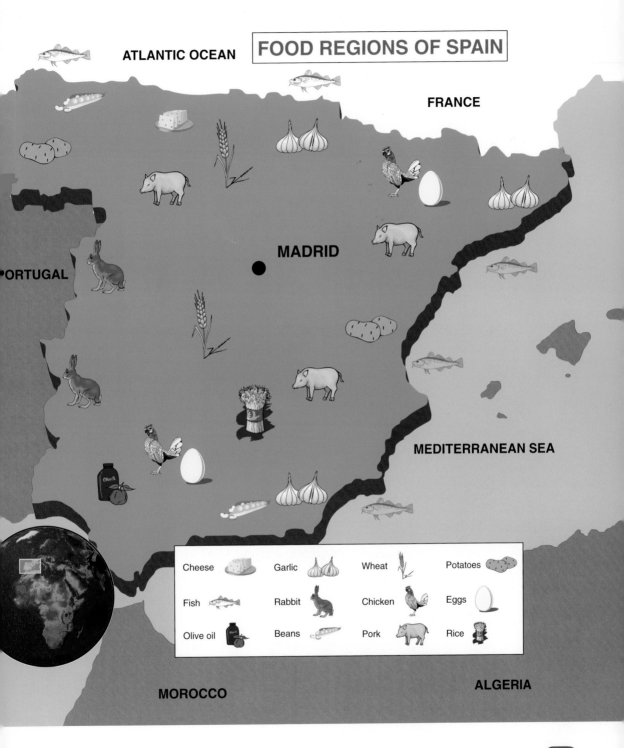

FOOD REGIONS OF SPAIN

ATLANTIC OCEAN

FRANCE

PORTUGAL

MADRID

MEDITERRANEAN SEA

Cheese		Garlic		Wheat		Potatoes	
Fish		Rabbit		Chicken		Eggs	
Olive oil		Beans		Pork		Rice	

MOROCCO

ALGERIA

Fresh Healthy Ingredients

5

Olive groves are found throughout Spain.

Olive oil varies in color and taste depending on the variety of olive it comes from.

olive trees in Spain 3,000 years ago. Today, 262 varieties of olives grow in groves throughout Spain. In fact, the Spanish region of Andalusia (ahn-dah-lou-see-ah) boasts more than 165 million olive trees, more than anywhere else in the world. Many of these trees are at least 100 years old.

Although Spaniards eat lots of olives, 90 percent of the olives grown here are used to make olive oil. Spanish olive oil varies in color and taste depending on the variety of olive it is extracted from. It can be green, pale yellow, or golden and can taste sweet, nutty, fruity, or slightly bitter. For instance, oil made from tiny

Arbequina (ar-bay-key-e-nah) olives is yellowish-green and tastes smooth and buttery, while the golden oil made from hojiblanco (ho-hee-blahn-coh) olives has a sweet fruity flavor.

The Flavor of Spain

Spanish cooks use olive oil in everything from main dishes to desserts, which may be why olive oil is often called the flavor of Spain. As a matter of fact, Spain is the world's largest consumer of olive oil. Each Spaniard uses about 30 pounds (3.62kg) of the rich oil annually. It is drizzled over cooked vegetables and grilled meat

Spanish Ham

Pork is an important staple in Spain. Iberico (e-bay-ree-co) ham is among everyone's favorites. It comes from pigs that are fed a special diet of acorns, which gives their meat a sweet nutty taste.

Iberico ham is preserved by a method known as air curing. The meat is rubbed with salt and left for several weeks. Next, the salt is washed off and the meat is hung to dry for up to three years. Although this is usually done in special facilities, in the past many Spanish homes had a loft room just for this purpose, and some farmhouses still do.

The ham is sliced thin and eaten uncooked as appetizers and snacks. Because it is so popular, many Spanish bars have dozens of hams in cradlelike frames called jamoneras (hah-moan-air-ahs) hanging from hooks in their ceiling. The meat is sliced as it is needed.

Making Olive Oil

To make olive oil, olives are placed in a metal-toothed grinder. It extracts the oil from the olives by squeezing or pressing them. Olives are put through the grinder many times. After each pressing, oil is extracted. Oil that has been through multiple pressings is used for cooking and frying. Extra-virgin olive oil, which is taken from the first pressing, is considered the finest olive oil. It is the oil that Spaniards dip bread in and use to dress their salads.

and fish. Cooks fry anything and everything in it. They make sauces and dressings with it. They use it in place of butter in baking. They flavor soups and mashed potatoes with it. They bathe salads in it. They dunk bread in it. In fact, a cruet of olive oil and little dipping bowls are found on almost every Spanish table. "Olive oil is mandatory at every meal in a Spanish home,"[1] explains Spanish chef Antonio Diaz. It adds a rich taste and aroma to Spanish cooking.

A Healthy Food

Spaniards not only enjoy the flavor of olive oil, but they also believe that eating olive oil keeps them healthy. And they may be right. Scientists say a diet rich in olive oil protects people from heart disease. That may be why the incidence of heart disease among Spanish women is the lowest in the world and why the

Garlic, along with olive oil, plays an important role in Spanish cooking.

Spanish people, in general, have one of the longest life expectancies on Earth.

Food and Medicine

Garlic is another important staple in Spanish cooking. Like olive oil, it not only tastes delicious, but it is also quite wholesome. For centuries, Spaniards considered it a cure-all and used the pungent herb not only to flavor food, but also to fight infection, treat respiratory and digestive illnesses, and repel evil spirits. Although garlic cannot do all these things, scientists have found that it has antibacterial properties and can indeed help fight infections. And when it is combined with olive oil, it releases a chemical that keeps blood clots from forming, which prevents heart attacks.

While Spaniards appreciate garlic's medicinal value, it is the delicious flavor and aroma it adds to food that they adore. Three types of garlic grow in Spain: white, pink, and yellow. White is the strongest tasting, while pink is the mildest. Pink is the most popular garlic in Spain.

Spanish cooks use garlic in a myriad of ways. It is pickled, roasted, fried, and eaten raw in salads. One

Garlic soup is a simple, aromatic soup that has been made for centuries.

Tomato Bread

Instead of buttering bread, Spaniards like to top bread with olive oil, garlic, and tomato. It tastes best if eaten while the bread is warm.

Ingredients
4 slices Italian or other crusty bread
4 teaspoons extra-virgin olive oil
2 small ripe tomatoes, cut in half
2 garlic cloves, cut in half
pinch of salt

Instructions
1. Toast the bread in a toaster oven or on a grill.
2. Rub each slice of bread with a garlic half.
3. Rub each slice of bread with a tomato half. Squeeze the tomato so that the juice and pulp get on the bread.
4. Sprinkle each slice of bread with a teaspoon of olive oil.

Serves 4.

Instead of buttered toast, Spaniards prefer toast flavored with garlic, tomato, and olive oil.

of their favorite uses is in garlic soup. Spaniards have been eating this simple fragrant soup for centuries. It is made with water, garlic, and olive oil, then topped with a poached egg and toasted bread and served in traditional earthenware bowls known as **cazuelas** (cahs-way-lahs).

Garlic is also the chief ingredient in **alioli** (ahl-ee-ol-ee) and **sofrito** (so-free-toe), two sauces that Spaniards love. Sofrito is made with garlic, olive oil, and tomatoes. Similar to tomato sauce, it adds a sweet zesty flavor to stews and rice dishes.

Alioli has a mayonnaise-like color and texture. The sauce is made by whisking olive oil with garlic, and it has a strong garlic flavor. Spaniards dip fried fish and seafood in it, marinate grilled foods in it, and dress potatoes with it. Says chef Marimar Torres: "It enhances grilled meat and fish, and can also enliven the flavor of a dish by stirring in just a spoonful at the end."[2]

Fish and Seafood

With 3,000 miles (4,828km) of coastline, Spain is blessed with an abundance of fish and seafood, important staples of the Spanish diet. In fact, Spaniards eat about 66 pounds (29.9kg) of fish and seafood per person annually. Since fish and seafood contain nutrients that fight heart disease, they contribute to the Spanish people's good health. But it is the simple and delicious flavor that Spaniards adore. "Spain . . . is a fish lover's

Garlic Shrimp

Garlic shrimp is a popular Spanish seafood dish.

Ingredients
24 medium shrimps, cleaned and peeled
4 garlic cloves, peeled and sliced
1 teaspoon red pepper flakes
¼ cup olive oil
1 tablespoon fresh parsley or cilantro, chopped
1 tablespoon lemon juice

Instructions
1. Heat the oil in a skillet. Add the shrimp, garlic, and red pepper flakes and cook on high heat until the shrimp are cooked, about 3–4 minutes. They should be pink and cooked throughout. Add the lemon juice.
2. Transfer the shrimp into a serving bowl and pour the oil and garlic over the shrimp. Sprinkle with parsley.

Serves 4.

Garlic shrimp is made from Spain's plentiful shrimp supply.

Because of the country's long coastline and plentiful catches, seafood plays an important part in Spanish meals.

Fresh fish markets are abundant in Spain. People demand—and get—only the freshest seafood.

paradise," explains chef Penelope Casas. "Fish reigns supreme and is the focus of all eating."[3]

Favorites include tuna, shrimp, cod, tiny eels that are as small as a baby's finger, bass, lobsters, hake, scallops, shrimp, octopus, and sardines, to name just a few. These may be grilled, baked, or fried. They may be bathed in olive oil and garlic, topped with sofrito or alioli, tossed in a salad, cooked with rice, or made into soup or stew. Cod is often dried and salted. This is known as **bacalao** (bahk-al-ow), which has been a Spanish favorite for centuries.

Fresh and Succulent

Because only the freshest products will do, rather than using a shopping list, Spaniards choose fish and seafood based on whatever has been harvested from the sea most recently. In coastal towns and cities, people can buy freshly caught fish and seafood right off fishing trawlers. Often the fishermen grill the fish in front of hungry customers. Manu, who grew up in a Spanish fishing village, recalls: "The only way we ate fish was off the boat. Next day we threw it out because for us it wasn't fresh."[4]

Fresh products are shipped to inland cities at least once a day. Freshness is so important that it is not uncommon for waiters in Spain's most elegant restaurants to bring uncooked fish to patrons to inspect before they place their order. When fish and seafood are newly caught, any way they are prepared tastes delicious. "The trick is to get the freshest fish and other natural ingredients and then use your imagination,"[5] says chef Jose Grimaldi.

By combining freshly caught fish and seafood, local olive oil, and garlic, Spanish cooks create healthy, simple, and delicious meals. These ingredients give Spanish cuisine its distinctive flavor and contribute to the good health and long life expectancy of the Spanish people.

Chapter 2

A Reflection of Geography and History

Because Spaniards prefer eating fresh local food, Spain's diverse geography and climate, which ranges from snow-capped mountains to hot sun-drenched beaches, affects what people eat. For instance, thick stews and soups are popular in the mountains. Fish pies made with cold-water creatures like octopus and cod are favored along the Atlantic coast, while along the Mediterranean coast, shellfish stews rule.

Despite these regional differences, all Spanish cooking reflects the nation's long colorful history. Favorite dishes such as **paella** (pah-el-yah), **gazpacho** (gahs-pah-cho), and **tortilla española** (tor-tee-ya es-pahn-yo-la) are good examples of this blending of history and location.

It Started with Rice

Paella is a rice dish that originated in Valencia, Spain, in the 19th century. But, if not for the ancient Romans and the **Moors**, this dish might never have been created.

The Moors were a group of Arabs who occupied Spain from the 8th to the 13th century. They were the first people to plant rice in Spain.

Spain's climate is somewhat dry for rice cultivation. But, because the Romans introduced irrigation farming to Spain 200 years earlier, this was not a problem. The Moors used this farming method to channel water from the mountains to the rice fields. Rice has flourished in Spain ever since.

Spanish Restaurants

Spaniards love to eat out. Rather than hosting dinner parties in their homes, it is common for Spaniards to invite guests to a restaurant.

Spaniards have been dining out for centuries. Many Spanish restaurants are more than 100 years old. In fact, the world's oldest restaurant is located in Madrid, Spain's capital. It was established in 1725.

Early Spanish restaurants began as taverns where travelers and local people came for a drink and a bite to eat. Many also provided rooms in which travelers could spend the night as well as stables for their horses.

Today, Spaniards eat about 50 pounds (22.7kg) of rice per person, per year. A large part of this is used in paella. Paella is a kind of stew that features a wide range of ingredients such as seafood, fish, pork, sausage, chicken, or rabbit. These may or may not be mixed with each other. There are seemingly limitless variations of the dish. "Put two Spanish cooks together and you'll likely get three paellas,"[6] say authors Richard Sterling and Allison Jones. But no matter the other ingredients, paella always contains rice, olive oil, sofrito, and **saffron**. The last is a costly spice that the Moors brought to Spain. Its bright yellow color brightens paella, and its tealike flavor adds a savory taste to the dish.

There are many variations of paella, but they always contains rice and saffron.

Saffron adds color and flavor to paella.

A Special Pan

Seafood paella is one of the most popular varieties. To make it, a mix of different seafood and fish are stir-fried in olive oil in a large round shallow pan, known as a **paellera** (pah-el-yare-ra). It has a handle on each side and a flat bottom, which helps distribute heat evenly.

Tomatoes, garlic, and onions, the ingredients that compose sofrito, come next, followed by the rice, which is seasoned with saffron. The whole thing is coated with more olive oil, and water or broth is added. As the paella cooks, the liquid is absorbed and the rice drinks in the flavors of the other ingredients.

The paella is done when a golden crust known as the soccarrat (so-cah-raht) forms on the bottom of the rice, while the rest of the rice is dry, plump, and slightly crunchy. Paella is usually served and eaten right out of the pan. Diners divide the paella up into sections and eat the delicious treat with special triangular spoons that are used only for this purpose.

The Paella Maestro

Although paella can be made on a stove, tradition-ally it is cooked outside over a wood fire made from orange-tree branches. This gives the dish a smoky taste and a citrusy fragrance. Because it is often cooked over an open fire, Spaniards say cooking paella is a man's job. As a matter of fact, men known as paella maestros

Cocido

Cocido (coh-cee-doh), which means *boiled* in Spanish, is a popular Spanish stew. It is made with chicken, beef, pork, sausage, and garbanzo beans, which are slowly cooked over low heat. Historians say that the first cocido was made by Spanish Jews hundreds of years ago. Because their religion prohibited them from working on the Sabbath, Jewish cooks prepared the stew before the Sabbath began and then left it to cook during the Sabbath.

Since Judaism also forbids eating pork, early cocido did not include it. In the 15th century, when Jews were forced to convert to Christianity or leave Spain, pork was added to the dish. By doing this, former Jews hoped to prove that they had truly given up their former religion.

Paella cooked outside in a large pan called a paellera can feed many people.

Gazpacho is a hearty soup served cold and is especially delicious on a hot day.

(pah-el-ya mah-es-tros) travel all over Spain cooking paella at festivals and other large gatherings. Paella maestros typically use huge paelleras in which they can cook enough paella to serve hundreds of people. For instance, a 52-inch (130cm) paellera makes enough paella to serve 200 people. Indeed, the largest paella ever made fed 50,000 people.

Whether paella is made for one person or a thousand, its delicious taste, enticing aroma, and colorful appearance makes it one of Spain's most popular and most famous foods. "Paella," explains an article in *Art Culinare* magazine, "transforms simple rice . . . into a complex and extraordinary meal."[7]

Liquid Salad

Gazpacho is another favorite dish that reflects Spain's rich past. It is a cold vegetable soup often described as "liquid salad." Its primary ingredients, tomatoes and bell peppers, were never seen in Spain, or the rest

Gazpacho

Making gazpacho with a blender is not difficult. It is important to chill the soup before serving it to allow the flavors to develop.

Ingredients
3 soft ripe tomatoes, chopped
1 clove of garlic, peeled and minced
½ sweet bell pepper (red, yellow, or orange), stem and seeds removed, chopped
½ small cucumber, peeled and chopped
¼ small red onion, chopped
3 cups tomato or vegetable juice
1 tablespoon extra-virgin olive oil
1 tablespoon red wine vinegar
½ cup croutons

Instructions
1. Put the vegetables and garlic in a blender and puree until no large pieces remain. You may have to do this a little at a time.
2. Add the juice, olive oil, and vinegar. Mix well with a spoon or in the blender.
3. Put gazpacho in a container and chill overnight.
4. Top with croutons before serving.

Serves 4.

Gazpacho is a cold vegetable soup often called a "liquid salad" because of its ingredients.

of Europe, until the 15th century. That was when Spanish explorers brought these vegetables, which are native to the Americas, to Spain. Before this time, gazpacho was a plain-tasting soup that consisted of stale bread, olive oil, garlic, and vinegar. Once tomatoes and bell peppers were added, gazpacho became the zesty red soup that Spaniards love.

In the past, making gazpacho was hard work. Cooks made a thick paste by pounding moist bread, garlic, onions, bell peppers, fresh vine-ripened tomatoes, vinegar, and olive oil with a **pestle**. To eliminate big pieces, the mixture was then pushed through a sieve.

Most modern cooks create smooth creamy gazpacho with a blender. Sometimes ground almonds, which were brought to Spain by the Moors, are added to the mixture to sweeten and thicken it. Or they are used in place of tomatoes to make white gazpacho. Green fava beans and lettuce are other possible ingredients.

Once the gazpacho is made, it is placed in the refrigerator to chill overnight. The next day the soup is usually placed on the table in a colorful pitcher. Small bowls filled with toppings such as sliced cucumbers, croutons, diced onions, and slices of hard-boiled egg and ham accompany it. To make the whole process even simpler, Spanish supermarkets sell containers of gazpacho, just the way orange juice is sold in North America.

Spaniards eat gazpacho year-round, although it is especially popular in hot weather. Its refreshing taste

Tortilla española is a versatile dish that's easy to make. It can be eaten hot or cold, anytime, anywhere. And most people love it!

quenches the thirst and energizes the body. "There is absolutely nothing like it in the hot summer months, although it seems to be just as popular when the weather turns cold,"[8] says Penelope Casas.

A Delicious Omelet

Tortilla española is also popular year-round. This potato omelet, which is often called the national dish of Spain, has its roots in Spain's past. Although modern Spaniards love potatoes, the vegetables are not native to Europe. They were brought to Spain from Peru in 1537 by Spanish explorers. The Spanish people fell in love

Tortilla Española

Making tortilla española is not difficult, but flipping the omelet can be tricky.

Ingredients
4 small potatoes, peeled and sliced into thin rounds
4 eggs, beaten
1 small onion, cut into small pieces
¼ cup plus 2 tablespoons olive oil
pinch of salt and pepper

Instructions
1. Heat ¼ cup olive oil in an 8–10 inch frying pan.
2. Put the potatoes, onions, salt, and pepper in the pan and cook over medium-to-low heat until the potatoes are soft but not brown. Stir to prevent them from sticking.
3. Drain the potato mixture. Pour the eggs over the potatoes. Let it stand for 5 minutes.
4. Wipe out the frying pan. Heat the 2 tablespoons of olive oil. Add the egg-potato mixture. Cook on medium-to-low heat until the bottom is set and golden brown. While cooking, shake the pan so that the mixture does not stick.
5. Flip the tortilla by putting a plate that is larger than the pan over the pan and turning the pan over. If any parts of the tortilla stick to the skillet, remove and flip them with a spatula. Slide the tortilla back into the pan, add any parts that were flipped with the spatula, and cook another 3 minutes.

Serves 4.

with potatoes, and it was not long before tortilla española was created.

Tortilla española is a flat cakelike omelet. Indeed, in Spain the word tortilla refers to an omelet rather than a flat bread as it does in Mexico. To make the delicious dish, chefs slowly cook a layer of potatoes in fragrant olive oil with onions and garlic. When the potatoes are golden, the ingredients are removed from the pan and added to beaten eggs. The mixture is cooked in a skillet until the bottom is lightly browned, then it is flipped and cooked some more. The end result is fluffy, crisp, light, and filling.

Sliced in wedges like a pizza, tortilla española is eaten hot or cold, for breakfast and supper. Spanish schoolchildren carry it for snacks in their lunch boxes. And Spanish picnics would not be the same without it. But no matter when it is eaten, tortilla española is, according to Marita, a Spanish woman who loves to cook, "the jewel of the Spanish kitchen."[9]

Tortilla española, paella, and gazpacho are all jewels of Spanish cooking. Not only do they taste delicious, but they also remind the Spanish people of their long and rich history.

3

Round-the-Clock Treats

Spaniards eat round-the-clock. Breakfast is served around 7 A.M. A few hours later, Spaniards enjoy a midmorning snack. Lunch follows late in the afternoon. **Merienda** (may-ree-en-dah), a late afternoon snack, and **tapas** (tah-pahs), an evening minimeal, tide hungry Spaniards over until supper, which is not eaten until at least 9 P.M. Some night owls might even have a predawn snack. On Sundays, Spaniards indulge in special sweet treats.

Sociable Bites

Tapas are bite-sized appetizers that Spaniards adore. These little snacks not only prevent Spaniards from getting hungry during the long stretch from lunch

Tapas are small appetizers that are best enjoyed while socializing with groups of friends.

to supper, but they also bring fun-loving Spaniards together. Eating tapas is one of the most social of all activities in Spain. In fact, meeting friends over tapas is practically a national pastime. Sharing tapas makes sense, since it allows diners to sample a large variety of the little treats. "Congregating to enjoy tapas offers friends and colleagues the chance to eat, to drink . . . and to socialize," says food writer Andrea Greeley. "Besides," she explains, "tapas are best eaten in groups, giving both cook and patron a chance to appreciate innumerable dishes with many different flavors, textures and colors."[10]

Countless Varieties

A tapa can be as simple as a piece of cheese or as complex as a perfect miniature pie stuffed with seafood. It can be hot or cold, cooked or uncooked. Anything served in a small portion can be a tapa. There are grilled shrimps on **banderillas** (bahn-day-ree-yas), miniature skewers named for the poles used in bull-fighting. And there are tiny fried baby squid that are so small and tender that they can be eaten in one bite, tentacles and all. Also popular are sausages rolled in cabbage leaves, pork rolled in ham, eggs stuffed with salmon, and little round turnovers and pies known as **empanadillas** (em-pahn-ah-dee-yas). These may be stuffed with tuna fish, sardines, meat, ham, or cheese. There are fried patties made of shrimp, clam, chicken, or even leftover paella. Small chunks of cheese, sausage, or olives wait to be speared with toothpicks or piled on bite-sized sandwiches. Tiny cazuelas are filled with stews, casseroles and soups, or seafood dripping with garlic and olive oil. Chunks of crusty bread are used to sop up the sauce. The choices are almost endless.

Some **tascas** (tah-scahs), the barlike restaurants where tapas are served, offer as many as 50 different kinds of tapas. Others specialize in a particular type of tapa. Spaniards often go from one tasca to another seeking their favorites. This is known as tasca hopping. But no matter which tapas diners select or where they go to find them, one thing is certain, the tapas are always freshly made right on the premises.

An Informal Place

Tascas are informal places. Spaniards have been coming to them for centuries. The first tascas were dusty roadside taverns where 18th-century travelers stopped for a drink. The tavern keeper often covered the drink with a slice of bread or ham, in order to keep dust and flies out. These bits of food were the first tapas. In fact, in Spanish, the verb "tapear" (tah-pay-are) means to cover.

Modern tascas are equally casual. Some have menus, while others list their fare on a large blackboard or simply spread their offerings on a long bar. Most tascas have a few small tables and chairs. But since they are often extremely crowded, it is common to dine standing at the bar. Friendly Spaniards do not seem to mind

Marinated Garbanzo Beans

Garbanzo beans, or chickpeas, are popular in Spain. This dish is a common tapa. It is tasty and easy to make. Sliced tomatoes and black olives can be added.

Ingredients
1 can (15 oz.) garbanzo beans
2 tablespoons red wine or balsamic vinegar
1 hard-boiled egg, chopped
¼ cup olive oil
2 tablespoons minced parsley or cilantro
1 tablespoon minced garlic
salt and pepper to taste

Instructions
1. Cook the beans as directed on the can. Drain in a colander.
2. Put the beans in a large bowl. Add the remaining ingredients and mix well.
3. Cover the bowl. Refrigerate overnight.

Serves 4.

Banderillas

Most anything that can be stuck on a wooden skewer or a toothpick can be a banderilla. Possible choices include an olive, a chunk of cheese, and a red bell pepper square; a piece of melon and a piece of ham; or a chunk of tuna fish, an olive, and a potato cube. This recipe uses shrimp, red pepper, olives, and cucumber. Tuna, ham, or cheese can be substituted for shrimp.

Ingredients
12 bamboo skewers, 6–9 inches in length
12 pimento-stuffed green olives
12 small cooked shrimps
1 red bell pepper, cleaned and cut into chunks
1 cucumber, peeled and cut into 12 rounds

Instructions
1. Put an olive, a shrimp, a pepper chunk, and a cucumber round on each skewer.

Serves 4.

Shrimps are only one of the many food items that can be used. If it can be skewered, it can be a banderilla.

the crowded atmosphere. The more diners, the more chance for lively conversations. And although tascas are considered bars where adults often drink wine with their tapas, families with children are a common sight. *Saveur* magazine editor Margo True, who lived in Spain as a child, recalls: "One of the things we'd do . . . was to go out at night and eat tapas with friends. . . . We use to call it tasca hopping, and what fun it was! We'd go into the most promising looking place and sit at a thick wooden table. . . . Then came the tapas, which seemed to me to be proportioned just right for a kid. We'd eat shrimp grilled in the shell, garlicky onions,

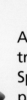

Heavenly Treats

Although cookies, cakes, and other pastries are available in bakeries throughout Spain, many Spaniards insist that the best pastries can be found at the country's 200 Catholic convents. Here, nuns who rarely go beyond the convent's walls bake and sell sweets in order to help pay for their lives of prayer.

Visitors give their orders at a special window. A nun, who can be heard but not seen, takes the order. The visitor pays for the sweets by placing money on a torno (tor-no), a round spinning tray. The nun spins the torno to get the money and then places the sweets on the torno for the customer.

Spanish nuns have been baking and selling pastries in this manner since the 15th century. Many use ancient recipes that have been passed down in their particular convent but kept secret from the public.

Spain produces many different cheeses made with milk from cows, sheep, or goats.

red capsicums [peppers], and always tortilla española. . . . I also remember that there were always plenty of kids running around."[11] Tapas are followed by a light supper.

Sweet Treats

Desserts eaten after lunch or supper are usually quite simple. Fresh fruit, rice pudding, or a baked custard known as **flan** (flahn) are common favorites. Pastries and sweet breads are reserved for merienda, as well as for breakfast. Sweets are also a frequent treat on Sunday when Spaniards flock to pastry shops to buy tarts and cakes to share with visiting family members.

No matter what the day or the time, hot chocolate is always popular. Spaniards drink it for breakfast, as part of a midmorning snack, in place of coffee or tea for merienda, and as a delicious end to late-night festivities. Spaniards have loved hot chocolate ever since the Aztec chief Montezuma served the Spanish explorer, Hernán Cortés, the drink in 1519. A year later Cortés introduced it to Spain.

Spanish Cheese

A chunk of cheese is a popular tapa. Spain produces about 100 different types of cheese, most of which are unfamiliar to North Americans. Spanish cheeses can be made with milk from cows, sheep, or goats.

Manchego (mahn-chay-go), a hard salty cheese made from sheep's milk, is one of the most well-known Spanish cheeses. Manchego is made in a special mold, which imprints a zigzag pattern on the sides of the cheese. A wooden board pressed on the top adds a wheat pattern.

Cabrales (cah-brah-lays) is another popular cheese. It is a blue cheese made from cow's milk. It is aged in a cave for three months. This produces the blue veins that run through the cheese and its strong scent.

Mahon (mah-hown) has a sweeter scent. It is also a cow's milk cheese. It is encased in a waxy red rind, which is rubbed with olive oil. This gives the sharp-tasting cheese a fruity aroma.

Early hot chocolate had a bitter taste, so Spanish cooks added sugar to sweeten it. The resulting drink became so popular that Spanish clergymen worried that it might be addictive. Despite these concerns, by the 17th century drinking hot chocolate had become so fashionable that Spanish royalty often hosted meriendas in which hundreds of guests were served hot chocolate flavored and scented with dried rosebuds, accompanied by sponge cake and other sweets.

Although modern Spanish hot chocolate rarely is made with rosebuds, it is different from that served in North America. Spanish hot chocolate tastes something like syrup made from a dark chocolate bar. It is dark brown, bittersweet, and so thick that it is similar to pudding in texture. The flavor, according to Anya von Bremzen, is "completely bewitching."[12]

Fried Dough

Hot chocolate is almost always accompanied by **churros** (chew-rros). Churros are thin fluted dough strips that are deep-fried in olive oil. Crisp on the outside and soft on the inside, churros go perfectly with hot chocolate. In fact, because churros are not very sweet, Spaniards like to dip them in sugar and then in their hot chocolate, giving the crispy pastry a yummy chocolate coating.

To make churros, dough made from flour, water, and olive oil is forced through a **churrera** (chew-rair-rah) a star-shaped tube similar to a pastry bag that gives the pastry its fluted edges. The dough is then fried in a vat

Hot chocolate and churros are an *irresistible* combination.

of hot bubbling oil until the churro is golden on the outside and tender within.

Churros may be plain or filled with cream. Either way, they are always eaten warm. Little cafés that specialize in churros and mobile carts known as churro stands are found on almost every busy city street and at all Spanish festivals. They fill the air with a tantalizing aroma. In the past, churro stands were a common sight on roadsides, where hungry travelers could stop and get a snack.

Today, Spaniards do not have to travel to satisfy their hunger for churros. With crispy churros, thick rich hot chocolate, and dozens of different varieties of tapas to tempt them, it is no wonder Spaniards eat day and night. These delectable treats are hard to resist.

chapter

4

Special Foods for Special Days

Spaniards celebrate their favorite holidays with special foods, many of which the Spanish people have been eating for centuries. Treats like **turron** (toor-rown), **rosca de reyes** (roh-scah day ray-yes), and **torrijas** (tor-ree-has) are beloved and traditional parts of holiday celebrations.

A Classic Christmas Treat

Christmas is a festive time in Spain. Street vendors sell hot roasted chestnuts that fill the air with a delicious aroma. Bakeries and sweet shops are filled with flaky pastries, crumbly biscuits, spongy cakes, and delicious jams that are eaten during the holiday season. What is served

Turron is a fudgelike candy of almonds and honey that has been made for 1,000 years. For most Spaniards, Christmas wouldn't be the same without it.

for Christmas dinner varies by region and may feature sweet almond soup, turkey, roast lamb or pork, bacalao, crabs, or lobster. But no matter what else is served, in Spain, Christmas would not be Christmas without turron. Spaniards consume 35,000 tons of the sweet every year, almost all of it during the Christmas season.

Turron is a fudgelike candy made from almonds, honey, sugar, and egg whites that Spaniards have been eating for about 1,000 years. The origins of the delectable sweet are uncertain. Historians believe that the Moors, who were known to make a paste of almonds, which is the basis for turron, created the feather-light confection. And, since honey and almonds have been symbols of good luck and prosperity since ancient times, the delicacy became associated with Christmas. In fact, turron has been a part of Spanish Christmas celebrations for so long that in 1584 when the Japanese ambassador visited Spain during the holiday, he was served the traditional sweet. An article on Spain-recipes.com, a Web site dedicated to Spanish cooking, explains, "without a doubt the consumption of turron is intimately linked to the Christmas season in Spain and it could be said that turrones are essential in the menus of these celebrations."[13]

Special cooks, who are considered highly skilled craftspeople, use ancient recipes that have been passed down for generations to create the confection. These cooks are members of 30 families who produce all the commercially available turron in Spain. To make the sweet treat, the ingredients are

Fruit compote can be made with practically any fruit. It can be served right away or put up in jars as gifts.

slowly cooked. When the mixture thickens and turns brown, it is placed in a rectangular or round wooden mold and left to cool.

The resulting confection can be hard or soft. Soft turron is made in the Spanish city of Jijona (hee-ho-nah), while the hard variety is made in Alicante (ah-lee-cahn-tay). These two cities have been the world capitals of turron production for 500 years. Turron is so important to these cities that there is a turron museum in Jijona

Fruit Compote

A compote is composed of stewed fruit cooked in syrup. Many Spaniards serve a fruit compote for Christmas dinner. It may feature one fruit such as pears, apples, or peaches, or it may be composed of a number of different fruits, including figs, prunes, raisins, and cherries. This compote features pears and apples.

Ingredients
2 apples, peeled and cut in chunks
2 pears, peeled and cut in chunks
¾ cup sugar
2 cups water
2 cinnamon sticks

Instructions
1. Place all ingredients in a pot and bring to a boil. Lower the heat and simmer for about 10 minutes until the fruit is soft.
2. Put the fruit in little bowls. Remove the cinnamon sticks. Pour the syrup over the fruit. Serve warm.

Serves 4–6.

with exhibits on the history of the sweet. Museumgoers can visit the factory and see soft turron being made. Because it contains minced almonds, it is light and fluffy. Whole almonds make hard turron crackly and crunchy.

Earning a Gold Seal

Whatever the texture, turron is always made with locally grown almonds and orange blossom or rose-

In Spain, the Christmas celebration runs through January 6, Three Kings Day.

Twelve Grapes

Eating twelve grapes on New Year's Eve is a Spanish tradition. At midnight, as clocks in city centers chime, celebrants put one grape in their mouth for each clock chime. Everyone is supposed to have eaten all their grapes by the last chime, but they rarely do. The sight of friends and family with their mouths stuffed with grapes makes everyone laugh, which starts the new year off on a happy note.

This custom began centuries ago, when Spain had an especially large grape harvest. Rather than waste the grapes, the king gave them out to everyone to eat on New Year's Eve.

mary honey, which gives it an irresistible taste and fragrance. Only the finest ingredients in specific proportions will do. That is why the Spanish government carefully regulates turron. The best turron earns a gold seal. This proves that the sweet is composed of at least 60 percent nuts and 10 percent pure honey, and that only the highest quality ingredients have been used.

Traditionally, the nuts are almonds. But peanuts, hazelnuts, and pine nuts may be substituted. And although plain turron is very popular, chocolate, coconut, egg yolks, and candied fruit may be added. No matter the variety, according to food writer Brett Allan

King who lives in Madrid, "every Spaniard can expect their Christmas to include turron."[14]

The King's Crown

In Spain the Christmas season doesn't end on Christmas day. Presents are not exchanged until January 6, a day known as Three Kings Day. On this day, most Spaniards believe that three gift-bearing kings visited the Christ child more than 2,000 years ago. According to legend, every January 6 since then, these same kings travel to Spain on camels carrying gifts for Spanish children.

Saints' Bones

All Saints' Day, which falls on November 1, is another important Spanish holiday. On this day, Spaniards honor deceased love ones by visiting their graves.

They also commemorate the day with a delicious and interesting-looking sweet treat known as huesos de santos (way-sos day sahn-toes), which means saints' bones.

Huesos de santos are made from marzipan, a sticky white almond paste that can be sculpted into many shapes. For huesos de santos, the paste is formed into a hollow cylinder, similar to a piece of bone. Traditionally, the "bone" is filled with yellow cream, which resembles bone marrow, although chocolate is also used. Eating the treat honors deceased religious figures and family members, as well as reminding Spaniards of the sweetness of life.

Rosca de reyes is a delicious sweet bread that is eaten on Three Kings Day. It contains a surprise that is supposed to bring the finder good luck.

To celebrate the kings' arrival, people all over Spain eat rosca de reyes, which means the kings' round bread. Spaniards have been doing this for hundreds of years.

Rosca de reyes is a delicious spongy ring-shaped sweet bread that is said to resemble a king's crown. It is made from sweet yeast dough with ingredients such as flour, yeast, eggs, sugar, grated lemon rind, butter, and orange blossom water. The last is a liquid that is made from the essence of the orange flower. The incredibly fragrant bread ring, which looks like a giant doughnut, is decorated with colorful candied fruit and silvery almonds. The decorations resemble the jewels on a royal crown.

Rosca de reyes may be plain or filled with cream, chocolate, or syrup. Regardless of what else it contains, the perfumed ring always contains a surprise. This is usually a bean or a small ceramic figure. Finding the item is said to bring a person good luck.

The tradition of hiding a surprise in a bread or cake began with the ancient Romans. By the 3rd century, Spaniards were hiding a fava bean in rosca de reyes. It represented the Christ child. Over time, the surprise changed. In fact, 15th century Spanish royalty often hid a jewel inside the pastry, which the finder kept. Although modern Spaniards are not likely to find a precious gem in their rosca de reyes, its good taste is a treat in itself. And it is still fun to find the prize within. Marimar Torres recalls, "I remember, as a child . . . hoping to find the prized fava bean and goody. And I still keep in Spain my enviable collection of prizes gathered over the years."[15]

Spanish Toast

Easter is another important holiday in Spain. As with Christmas, Easter dinner varies throughout the country. There is only one dish that is eaten everywhere: torrijas.

Torrijas are slices of bread that are soaked in milk, sugar, and eggs. They originated in medieval Spain as

Torrijas

Torrijas are not difficult to make. Use thick crusty bread. The cooked torrijas can be topped with honey, jam, or syrup.

Ingredients
8 slices of Italian or other crusty bread
1 cup milk
½ cup sugar
2 eggs
¼ cup olive oil

Instructions
1. Put the milk and sugar in a pot and heat until the sugar dissolves.
2. Put the bread in a large bowl. Pour the milk mixture over the bread. Let the bread sit in the milk for 15 minutes.
3. Heat the oil in the frying pan.
4. In another bowl mix the eggs. Dip the bread in the eggs and fry in the oil, turning so both sides of the bread cooks. The torrijas are done when they are golden brown. If desired, torrijas may be rolled in more sugar before serving.

Serves 4–8.

a way to use stale bread. Because of their plentiful use of eggs, they became associated with Easter. This is because Christians consider Easter a time of religious rebirth, and throughout history the egg has been symbolic of new life.

Although torrijas are quite similar to French toast, food historians say that torrijas were created first. The first written recipe for the Spanish version goes back to 1599, while the first French recipe was not written until 60 years later. And there are differences in taste.

Torrijas are fried in olive oil rather than butter, which gives them a rich, fruity flavor. Once they are golden, diners dip them in sugar, cinnamon, wine, syrup, and/or honey, which adds variety to the basic crisp egg-and-bread flavor. The results are sweet and delectable. "You should definitely try torrijas at Easter," a chef at Spain-recipes.com, advises. "They are eaten all over Spain."[16]

Special holiday foods like torrijas, rosca de reyes, and turron are indeed eaten all over Spain. These traditional holiday treats have helped make Spanish holidays more memorable and fun for centuries and probably will continue to do so for many years to come.

Metric Conversions

Mass (weight)

1 ounce (oz.)	= 28.0 grams (g)
8 ounces	= 227.0 grams
1 pound (lb.) or 16 ounces	= 0.45 kilograms (kg)
2.2 pounds	= 1.0 kilogram

Liquid Volume

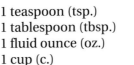

1 teaspoon (tsp.)	= 5.0 milliliters (ml)
1 tablespoon (tbsp.)	= 15.0 milliliters
1 fluid ounce (oz.)	= 30.0 milliliters
1 cup (c.)	= 240 milliliters
1 pint (pt.)	= 480 milliliters
1 quart (qt.)	= 0.96 liters (l)
1 gallon (gal.)	= 3.84 liters

Pan Sizes

8- inch cake pan	= 20 x 4-centimeter cake pan
9-inch cake pan	= 23 x 3.5-centimeter cake pan
11 x 7-inch baking pan	= 28 x 18-centimeter baking pan
13 x 9-inch baking pan	= 32.5 x 23-centimeter baking pan
9 x 5-inch loaf pan	= 23 x 13-centimeter loaf pan
2-quart casserole	= 2-liter casserole

Temperature

212° F	= 100° C (boiling point of water)
225° F	= 110° C
250° F	= 120° C
275° F	= 135° C
300° F	= 150° C
325° F	= 160° C
350° F	= 180° C
375° F	= 190° C
400° F	= 200° C

Length

1/4 inch (in.)	= 0.6 centimeters (cm)
1/2 inch	= 1.25 centimeters
1 inch	= 2.5 centimeters

Notes

Chapter 1: Fresh Healthy Ingredients

1. Quoted in Joan Raymund, "World's Healthiest Foods: Olive Oil (Spain)," Health.com, March 2006, www.health.com/health/artile/0,23414,1149135,00.html.

2. Marimar Torres, *The Spanish Table.* New York: Doubleday, 1986, p. 6.

3. Penelope Casas, *The Foods and Wines of Spain.* New York: Knopf, 2005, p. 220.

4. Quoted in Anya von Bremzen, *The New Spanish Table.* New York: Workman, 2005, p. 192.

5. Quoted in Richard Sterling and Allison Jones, *World Food Spain.* Victoria, Australia: Lonely Planet, 2000, p. 18.

Chapter 2: A Reflection of Geography and History

6. Sterling and Jones, *World Food Spain.* p. 59.

7. "Paella . . . More than Your Average Rice Dish—Back to Basics," *Art Culinare*, Fall 2003, www.findarticles.com/p/articles/mi_m0JAW/is_70/ai_109580396.

8. Casas, *The Foods and Wines of Spain.* p. 130.

9. Quoted in "Tortilla Española," ACocinar.com, www.acocinar.com/tortilla.htm. Quote translated by Barbara Sheen.

Chapter 3: Round-the-Clock Treats

10. Andrea Greeley, "Seduced by Tapas," *Vegetarian Times*, March 2004, www.findarticles.com/p/articles/mi_m0820/is_319/ai_113599724Seduced.

11. Quoted in Sterling and Jones, *World Food Spain*. p. 76.

12. Bremzen, *The New Spanish Table*. p. 425.

Chapter 4: Special Foods for Special Days

13. "Spanish Turron," Spain-recipes.com, http://www.spain-recipes.com/spanish-turron.html.

14. Quoted in Sterling and Jones, *World Food Spain*. p. 122.

15. Torres, *The Spanish Table*. p. 199.

16. "Torrijas," Spain-recipes.com, http://www.spain-recipes.com/torrijas.html.

Glossary

alioli: A mayonnaise-like sauce made with garlic and olive oil.

bacalao: Dried salted cod fish.

banderillas: Miniature skewers used to hold tapas.

cazuelas: Earthenware bowls.

churrera: A star-shaped tube used to shape churros.

churros: Fried pastries.

cuisines: The foods of a nation or a group of people.

empanadillas: Small stuffed turnovers and pies.

flan: A baked custard dessert.

gazpacho: A cold vegetable and bread soup.

merienda: A late afternoon snack.

Moors: The name of a group of Arabs who occupied Spain from the 8th to the 13th century.

paella: A rice dish that often features seafood.

paellera: A pan used to make paella.

pestle: A small club-like tool used to mash vegetables, herbs, and spices.

rosca de reyes: A cake that is traditionally eaten on January 6 to end the Christmas season.

saffron: A spice made from the crocus flower.

sofrito: A sauce made with garlic, olive oil, and tomatoes.

tapas: Bite-sized appetizers or snacks.

tascas: The barlike restaurants in which tapas are served.

torrijas: A bread and egg dish similar to French toast.

tortilla española: A potato omelet.

turron: A fudge-like sweet made from ground nuts.

For Further Exploration

Books

Joan D'Amico and Karen Eich Drummond, *The Science Chef Travels Around the World*. New York: Wiley, 1996. This book offers recipes from around the world, including Spain, with science experiments to go with the recipes.

Rebecca Christian, *Cooking the Spanish Way: Revised and Expanded to Include New Low-Fat and Vegetarian Recipes*. Minneapolis: Lerner, 2002. This is a Spanish cookbook for kids.

Lewis K. Parker, *Spain*, Discovering Cultures. New York: Benchmark, 2003. Looks at the history, geography, and culture of Spain.

Sue Townsend, *Spain*, World of Recipes. Chicago, Heinemann, 2003. A Spanish cookbook for kids.

Web Sites

Go Spain (www.gospain.org/index.html). A Web site with dozens of links providing all kinds of information about Spain, including Spanish cooking.

Kids.Net.Au "Spain: Encyclopedia," (www.kids.net.au/encyclopedia-wiki/sp/Spain). Gives information on

Spain's history, geography, government, famous people, and culture with links.

Notes from Spain (www.notesfromspain.com). A Web site geared to adults that provides information about life in Spain, including recipes, and podcasts about Spanish cooking.

Spain-Info.com (www.spain-info.com/index.html). This excellent Web site has maps and pictures and information about Spanish history, the flag, and culture. Included are facts about popular sports, bullfighting, and flamenco dancing.

Index

Picture credits

Cover: © Royalty Free/Corbis
AP Images, 48, 51
© David Bishop/Jupiter Images, 38
© Ross Durant/Jupiter Images, 12
© Alexandra Grablewski/Jupiter Images, 53
© Brian Hagiwara/Jupiter Images, 35
© 2007 Royalty Free/Shutterstock.com, 6, 7, 10,
       11, 14 15, 20, 21, 24, 28, 32, 36, 46
© 2007 Royalty Free/iStockphoto.com, 16, 23, 26,
       41, 44

About the Author

Barbara Sheen is the author of numerous books for young people, including more than 30 nonfiction books. She lives in New Mexico with her family. In her spare time, she likes to swim, walk, garden, and read. And, of course, she loves to cook!